by Michael Barrett and David Angerman

CONTENTS

4 All is Well (Prelude)
6 Prepare Ye the Way
(*with* "Shout to the North")
16 O Savior of Our Fallen Race
26 Promises of Isaiah
38 Breath of Heaven (Mary's Song)
50 Here I am to Worship
(*with* "O Come, All Ye Faithful")
60 One King
70 Light of the Stable
81 All is Well
88-96 optional instrumental parts

① This symbol indicates a track number on the StudioTrax CD (Accompaniment Only) or Split-Trax CD.

A Division of Shawnee Press, Inc.
Exclusively Distributed By Hal Leonard Corporation

Visit Shawnee Press Online at
www.shawneepress.com

PERFORMANCE NOTES

"All Is Well" offers two options for the narrations. One takes on a more dramatic approach while the other incorporates Scripture passages. Either is very effective and your choice may depend on what might best communicate to your particular congregation. Be free to adapt these as you wish.

THE WATCHMAN:

[underscore]

I am the watchman.

From ancient times I have gazed into the night
seeking the assuring light of the morning.

Walking the ramparts of the city wall,
I ring out the warning when danger threatens.

In the still of the night,
it is the sound of my voice that offers peace in the shadows.
Each hour I cry, "All is Well,"
until the silver stars of evening
surrender to the golden warmth of dawn.

I am the watchman.

From ancient times I have gazed into the Scripture
seeking the assuring promises of God.

Protecting the fortresses of faith I shout,
"Sleepers awake! Prepare the way of the Lord."

"All is Well! All is Well! The Son is coming soon!"

****

(optional alternative narration)

NARRATOR: *[underscore]*
Comfort my people, says our God. Comfort them! Encourage the people of Jerusalem. Tell them they have suffered long enough and their sins are now forgiven. I have punished them in full for all their sins.

A voice cries out, "Prepare in the wilderness a road for the Lord! Clear the way in the desert for our God! Fill every valley; level every mountain. The hills will become a plain, and the rough country will be made smooth. Then the glory of the Lord will be revealed, and all people will see it. The Lord Himself has promised this.
Isaiah 40:1-5 (GNT)

ALL IS WELL

(Prelude)

Arranged by
MICHAEL BARRETT (BMI)

Music by
MICHAEL W. SMITH
and WAYNE KIRKPATRICK

* Tune: STILLE NACHT, Franz Gruber, 1787-1863

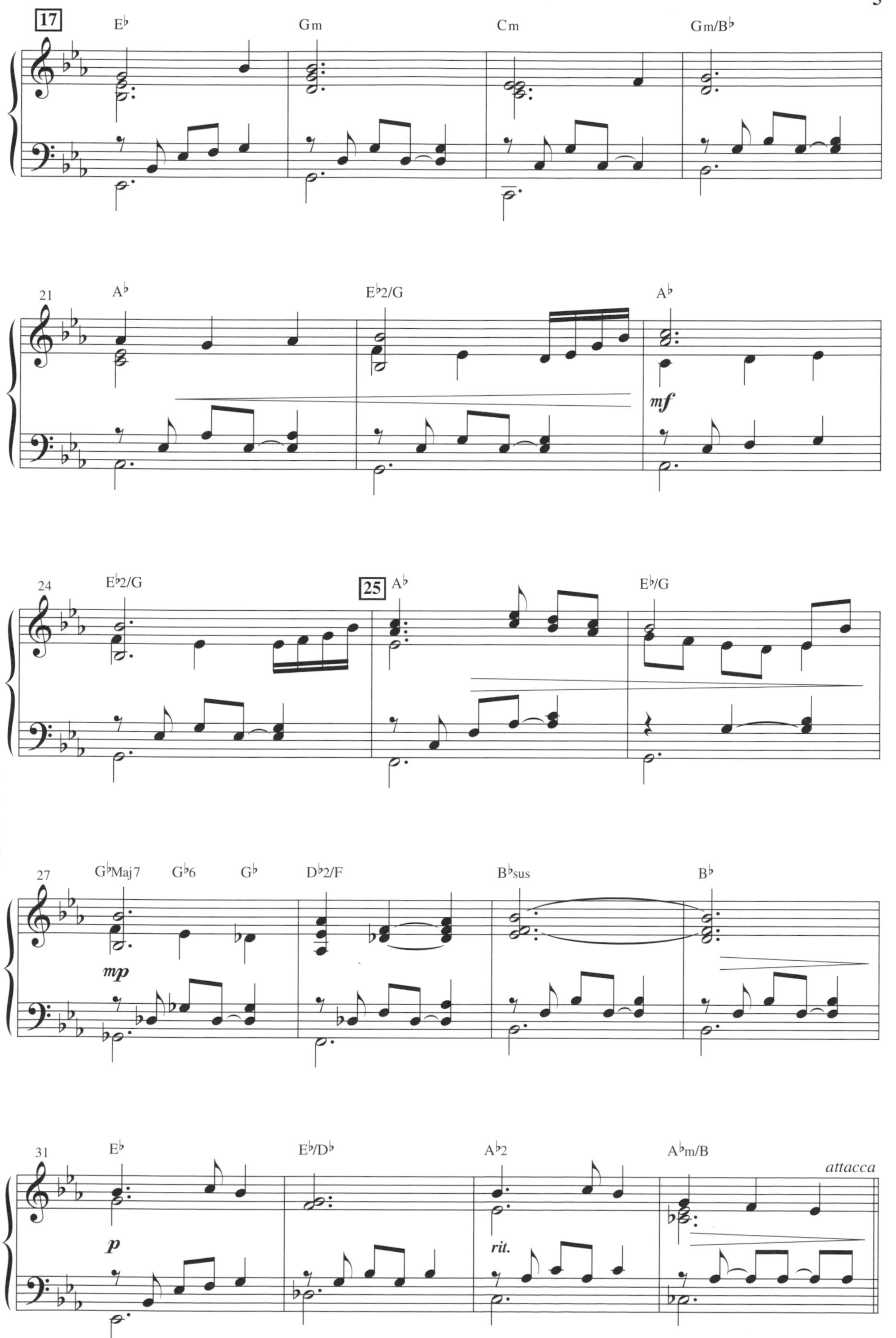
17
E♭
Gm
Cm
Gm/B♭
21
A♭
E♭2/G
A♭
mf
24
E♭2/G
25
A♭
E♭/G
27
G♭Maj7
G♭6
G♭
D♭2/F
B♭sus
B♭
mp
31
E♭
E♭/D♭
A♭2
A♭m/B
attacca
p
rit.

PREPARE YE THE WAY

(*with* "Shout To The North")

Arranged by
MICHAEL BARRETT (BMI)

"Prepare Ye the Way"
Words and music by
MICHAEL BARRETT (BMI)
"Shout to the North"
Words and music by
MARTIN SMITH

pare ye the way, the way of the Lord. Make straight in the des - ert a
B♭m7
E♭
Cm
Gm
high-way for God. Pre - pare ye the way of the Lord. Pre -
unis.
mf
A♭
E♭/G
Fm7
E♭/G
E♭
D♭
B♭sus
B♭
N.C.
pare ye the way, the way of the Lord Pre - pare ye the way, the
pare, pre-pare the way of the Lord. Pre - pare, pre-pare the
E♭
B♭m7
E♭
f
13

* alternate text

27
sing of the great and glo - rious King. You are
pare ye the way. Pre - pare ye the way.
A♭2 A♭ E♭ B♭ A♭ A♭2
30
strong when you feel weak; in your bro - ken - ness, com -
Pre - pare ye the way; in your bro - ken - ness, com -
E♭ B♭ A♭2 E♭ B♭
33
cresc.
plete.
Shout to the north and the south.
35
f
plete.
A♭ A♭2 E♭ A♭ E♭/A♭ B♭

* alternate text

48
hearts. Who can know the heal - ing pow'r of our
pare ye the way.
Pre - pare ye the way of our
B♭2
F
C
B♭2
51
awe - some King of love?
awe - some King of love.
F
C
B♭
B♭2
54
f
Shout to the north and the south. Sing to the
F
B♭
F/B♭
C
F

57
unis.
east and the west: Je - sus is Sav - ior to all,
unis.
57 B♭ F/B♭ C Dm7 Gm7 F/G C
60
62
Lord of heav - en and earth. Shout to the
60 Gm7 F/G Csus C F
62 F
mf
f
63
north and the south. Sing to the east and the west:
unis.
63 B♭ F/B♭ C F B♭ F/B♭ C

unis.
Je - sus is Sav - ior to all, Lord of heav - en and
Dm7 Gm7 F/G C Gm7 F/G Csus C
earth, Lord of heav - en and earth.
5
F C/E Dm Gm7 F/G Csus C F Cm7
mf cresc.
73
Pre - pare ye the way, the way of the Lord. Pre -
Shout! Sing! the way of the Lord.
F Cm7 F Cm7 F
f

75
pare ye the way the way of the Lord. Pre - pare ye the way, the
unis.
Shout! Sing! the way of the Lord. Shout! Sing!
75
F
Cm7
F
78
way of the Lord. Pre - pare ye the way. Pre - pare ye the way of the
78
Cm7
F
D♭
E♭
81
ff
Lord!
ff
81
F
E♭
F/D♭
E♭
F
N.C.
ff
2
2

THE WATCHMAN:

Day after day I stand on the watchtower.
Every night I stay at my post and wait.
When will the sorrow of my people end?
The children of Adam are crushed under the weight of sin.
They have forgotten that they are a gift of light from heaven.

They cry to me, "Watchman, what is left of the night?"

Morning is coming.
"Take heart and keep the watch," I tell them.
"See, a Redeemer approaches.
The dust of His chariot paints the horizon
with the colors of hope and promise."

The people who walk in darkness will see a great light.
On those living in the land of the shadow of death, a light will dawn.
A Savior will come and will shine with the brightness
of His Father's face.
He will be the very Light of Light, the Bright and Morningstar.
He will be the Son of God!

****

(optional alternative narration)

NARRATOR:

Everyone has sinned and is far away from God's saving presence. Sin came into the world through one man, and his sin brought death with it. As a result, death has spread to the whole human race because everyone has sinned.
Romans 3:23; Romans 5:12 (GNT)

For just as death came by means of a man, in the same way the rising from death comes by means of a man. For just as all people die because of their union with Adam, in the same way all will be raised to life because of their union with Christ.
1 Corinthians 15:21-22 (GNT)

O SAVIOR OF OUR FALLEN RACE

Words from "Christe Redemptor Omnium"
Latin office hymn, c. 6th Century
Translated by
GILBERT R. DOAN, JR. (1930)

Words and music by
KEITH *and* KRISTYN GETTY
Arranged by
DAVID ANGERMAN (ASCAP)

* Part for Oboe (or other C-Instrument) is on pages 88-89.

11
mf
fore the world knew day or night, O
13
Je - sus, ver - y Light of Light, our con-stant star in sin's deep night: Now
mf
- ob
+ ob
15
mp
hear the pray'rs Your peo - ple pray through - out the world this ho - ly
mp
17
(end solo)
7
day.
mf

21
mf unis.
Re - mind us Lord of life and grace, how
TENOR
mf unis.
BASS
- ob
+ ob
once, to save our fall - en race, You put our hu - man ves - ture
- ob
+ ob
on and came to us as Ma - ry's Son. To -

29
day, as year by year its light brings to our world a prom - ise
29
- ob
32
unis.
bright, one pre - cious truth out - shines the sun: Sal -
unis.
32
+ ob
35
8
va - tion comes from You a - lone.
35

38
39
f
unis.
For from the Fa-ther's throne You came, His
- ob
40
ban-ished chil-dren to re-claim; and earth and sea and sky re-vere the
42
43
love of Him who sent You here; and we are ju - bi - lant to - day, for
+ ob

44
unis.
You have washed our guilt a - way. O hear the glad new song we sing on
46
this, the birth of Christ, our King!
- ob
+ ob
dim. poco a poco
50
9
52
mp unis. (opt. solo)
O Sav - ior of our fall - en race, the
mp
Oo
mp

53
world will see Your ra - diant face, for You who came to us be - fore will
Oo
Oo
53
55
come a - gain and all re - store.
(end solo)
mp unis.
Let
Oo
55
57
songs of praise Your name a - dorn, O Christ, Re-deem-er, vir - gin - born, Whom
unis.
unis.
Oo
Oo
57

59

(10) *rit.*

with the Fa - ther we a - dore and Ho - ly Spir - it ev - er -

59

- ob

rit.

61

p

more.

p

62 *a tempo*

Al - le - lu, al - le - lu - ia.

Al - le -

61

62 *a tempo*

+ ob

p

63

dim. poco a poco al fine

Al - le - lu, al - le - lu - ia. Al - le - lu, al - le - lu - ia.

dim. poco a poco al fine

lu - ia. Al - le - lu - ia. Al - le -

63

dim. poco a poco al fine

65
S.
pp
Al - le - lu - ia. Al - le - lu.

A.
pp
Al-le-lu, al-le-lu - ia.___ Al-le-lu, al-le-lu - ia.___

T.B.
pp
lu - ia. Al - le - lu - ia. Al - le -

65
pp

67
ppp
Al - le - lu - ia. Al - le - lu - ia.

ppp
Al-le-lu, al-le-lu - ia.___ Al - le - lu - ia.

ppp
lu - ia. Al - le - lu - ia.

67
- ob
ppp
+ ob

THE WATCHMAN:

A righteous ruler is coming.

The government will rest upon His shoulders and He will be called
Wonderful Counselor,
Mighty God,
The Everlasting Father,
The Prince of Peace.

The dazzling light of heaven will shine in the hearts of the people
and the Word of the Lord will be revealed.

God will tabernacle *(dwell)* with His creation
and the whole world will be filled with His glory.
His kingdom of light will be firmly established and will never end!

This is the promise of God.

****

(optional alternative narration)

NARRATOR:
A Child is born to us! A Son is given to us! And He will be our ruler. He will be called, Wonderful Counselor, Mighty God, Eternal Father, Prince of Peace.

His royal power will continue to grow; His kingdom will always be at peace. He will rule as King David's successor, basing His power on right and justice, from now until the end of time. The Lord Almighty is determined to do all this.
Isaiah 9:6-7 (GNT)

PROMISES OF ISAIAH

Words by
MICHAEL BARRETT (BMI)

Music by
MICHAEL BARRETT (BMI)
and DAVID ANGERMAN (ASCAP)

* Part for 2 Flutes (or other C-Instruments) is on pages 94-96.

10
mf
us a Son is giv - en, and the
mf
a Son is giv - en. The
F G A B♭m6/A A
mf
13
gov - ern-ment shall be up - on His shoul - ders,
gov - ern-ment shall be, the gov - ern-ment shall
Gm7 C7 C FMaj7
- fl. 1&2
+ fl. 1
16
and the gov - ern-ment shall be up - on His
be,
B♭Maj7 Gm Gm6 Gm7/F Em7(♭5)
+ fl. 2
- fl. 1
- fl. 2
+ fl. 1&2

19
cresc.
21
f
shoul - ders, and His name shall be call - ed
Asus
A
F
B♭
C
22
Won-der - ful Coun-se - lor, Might - y God,
F2/4 F
Gm
C
F C F N.C.C F
D
26
mf
Ev - er - last - ing Fa - ther, Ev - er - last - ing
Gm7
C
F2
FMaj7
Em7(♭5)
A
fl. 1&2

29
mp
Fa - ther, the Might - y God, the Prince of
mp
29 D 2 4 Dm B♭ Gm6 Gm7 Gm6
+ fl. 1&2
mp
- fl. 1&2
32
mf
34
mp unis.
Peace. For un - to
mf unis.
32 A N.C. 34 Dm C/D
mf + fl. 2 + fl. 1
mp - fl. 1&2
35
us a Child is born, a Child is
mp
For un - to us a Child is
35 B♭Maj7 C Dm C/D B♭Maj7 C

* Tune: FRENCH CAROL

48
deem - er. Reign in maj - es - ty.
Dm B♭ Gm F/A D(no3) C(no3) D(no3) N.C. C(no3) D(no3)
- fl. 1&2
mp
+ fl. 1&2
51
52
mp
unis.
An - cient of Days, we crown You now with
N.C. Dm Gm6/B♭ A7 N.C. Dm Gm6/B♭
55
praise! Au - thor of cre - a - tion,
A Gm6/A Dm/A Am7 Dm G Dm B♭Maj7
- fl. 1&2

59

13

come and set us free.

59 B♭6 Dm/A A Dm Dm/C B7sus B7

+ fl. 1 + fl. 2

62

mf

For un - to us a Child is born,

mf

For un - to

62 Em Bm7 Em Bm7 Em Bm7

mf

65

for un - to us a Son is

us a Child is born,

65 Em Bm7 Em G A

68
70
giv - en, and the gov - ern-ment shall
a Son is giv - en.
B
Am6/B
B
Am7
- fl. 1&2
71
be up - on His shoul - ders, and the
unis.
The gov - ern-ment shall be,
D
G
CMaj7
+ fl. 1
+ fl. 2
74
gov - ern-ment shall be up - on His shoul - ders,
cresc.
Am
Am6
Am7
Am/F♯
Am6/F♯
Am7/F♯
Am/F♯
Bsus
- fl. 1
- fl. 2
+ fl. 1
+ fl. 2

77
78
f
and His name shall be call - ed Won - der - ful
B G C D G 2/4 G
80
Coun - se - lor, Might - y God,
Am D G D/G N.C. D/G G E
83
Ev - er - last - ing Fa - ther, Ev - er - last - ing
Am D G F♯7(♭5) B
- fl. 1&2

Fa - ther, the Might - y God, the Prince of
E4/2 Em C Am7 Am7 Am6
+ fl. 1&2
- fl. 1&2
Peace.
B N.C. Em D/E CMaj7 D
+ fl. 2 + fl. 1
14
95
mp unis.
For un - to
Em D/E CMaj7 D
95 Em D/E

96
us a Child is born,
mp unis.
For un - to us a Child is
96 CMaj7 D Em D/E CMaj7 D
- fl. 1&2
99
rit.
p a Child is
for un - to us a Child is born, a Child is,
born,
99 Em D/E C D CMaj7 D2
rit.
p
+ fl. 2 + fl. 1
103 born.
a Child is born.
p
103 N.C. Em Am/E D2/E E

THE WATCHMAN:

Listen to my words people of promise.

Be filled with the spirit of hope,
for God Himself shall give you a sign.
Behold, a virgin shall conceive, and bear a Son,
and shall call His name Immanuel –
"God With Us!"
In a small village this maiden will deliver her Child
and He will be the ruler of heaven and earth.

This will be a great miracle –
the sacred moment the world has longed and prayed for.

This gentle young woman will hold the future in her arms
and cradle the very Son of God close to her heart.

****

(optional alternative narration)

NARRATOR:
The Lord Himself will give you a sign: a young woman who is pregnant will have a Son and will name Him Immanuel.
Isaiah 7:14 (GNT)

God sent the angel Gabriel to a town in Galilee named Nazareth. He had a message for a young woman promised in marriage to a man named Joseph, who was a descendant of King David. Her name was Mary. The angel came to her and said, "Peace be with you! The Lord is with you and has greatly blessed you! You will become pregnant and give birth to a Son, and you will name Him Jesus. He will be great and will be called the Son of the Most High God. The Lord God will make Him a King, as His ancestor David was, and He will be the King of the descendants of Jacob forever; His kingdom will never end!"

"I am the Lord's servant," said Mary; "may it happen to me as you have said." And the angel left her.
Luke 1:26-28,31-32,38 (GNT)

BREATH OF HEAVEN

(Mary's Song)

Arranged by
MICHAEL BARRETT (BMI)

Words and music by
AMY GRANT
and CHRIS EATON

* Tune: COVENTRY CAROL, Traditional English melody

13
mp
wea - ry with a Babe in - side, and I
15
mp
won - der what I've done. Ho-ly
17
3
Fa - ther, You have come and cho - sen me
19
3
p
(end solo)
now to car - ry Your Son.
p

16
22
mp I am wait - ing in a
Oo
TENOR / BASS
mp
mp
si - lent prayer. I am fright - ened by the
si - lent prayer. Oo
load I bear.
load I bear. In a world as cold as
unis.
as

27
stone,
must I walk this path a -
cold as stone,
the
29
3
unis.
lone?
Be with me now.
Be with me
path a - lone?
Lord, be with me
31
17
p
32
mf
Breath of Heav - en, hold me to-
now.

33
geth - er. Be for - ev - er near me, Breath of
35
Heav - en, Breath of Heav - en, light-en my
37
unis.
dark - ness. Pour ov-er me Your ho - li-ness, for You are

39
mp
ho - ly,
Breath of
39
mp
41
Heav - en.
41
43
18
mp
44
Do You won - der as You
mp unis.
43
44
mp

45
watch my face, if a wis - er one should have
47
had my place? But I of - fer all I
unis.
I
49
am, for the mer - cy of Your
of - fer who I am,

51
unis. (opt. solo)
plan. Help me be strong. Help me
53
19
(end solo)
be. Help me.
55
p
Breath of Heav - en, hold me to - geth - er. Be for - ev - er

57
near me, Breath of Heav - en,
57
59
mp
Breath of Heav - en, light-en my dark - ness. Pour ov-er me Your
mp
59
mp
61
20
ho - li-ness, for You are ho - ly.
61

64
f
Breath of Heav - en, hold me to - geth - er. Be for - ev - er
f
64
f
66
near me, Breath of Heav - en.
66
68
f
Breath of Heav - en, light-en my dark - ness. Pour ov-er me Your
f
68
f

70
dim. poco a poco
ho - li - ness, for You are ho - ly. You are
dim. poco a poco
70
dim. poco a poco
72
rit.
p
ho - ly, You are ho ly, ho - ly,
p
72
rit.
p
75
Slowly
pp
Breath of heav - en.
pp
75
Slowly
pp

THE WATCHMAN:

Sleepers Awake!
Arise and shine for your light has come!

The Glory of the Lord is now made known to you.
Legions of angels are proclaiming the news
of peace and goodwill to all creation.
The hills and valleys that once rang
with the sounds of war and conflict
all echo with praise and thanksgiving.

Sleepers Awake!
Follow all seekers of light to Bethlehem
and worship the newborn King.

Let the wonder take you!
Let the miracle surround you.

Sleepers Awake!
Give yourself to praise!

****

(optional alternative narration)

NARRATOR:
She gave birth to her first Son, wrapped Him in cloths and laid Him in a manger – there was no room for them to stay in the inn.

There were some shepherds in that part of the country who were spending the night in the fields, taking care of their flocks. An angel of the Lord appeared to them, and the glory of the Lord shone over them. They were terribly afraid, but the angel said to them, "Don't be afraid! I am here with good news for you, which will bring great joy to all the people. This very day in David's town your Savior was born – Christ the Lord! And this is what will prove it to you: you will find a baby wrapped in cloths and lying in a manger."

Suddenly a great army of heaven's angels appeared with the angel, singing praises to God: "Glory to God in the highest heaven, and peace on earth to those with whom He is pleased!"

When the angels went away from them back into heaven, the shepherds said to one another, "Let's go to Bethlehem and see this thing that has happened, which the Lord has told us."
Luke 2:7-15 (GNT)

HERE I AM TO WORSHIP

(*with* "O Come, All Ye Faithful")

Arranged by
DAVID ANGERMAN (ASCAP)

Words and music by
TIM HUGHES
Incorporating
"O Come, All Ye Faithful"

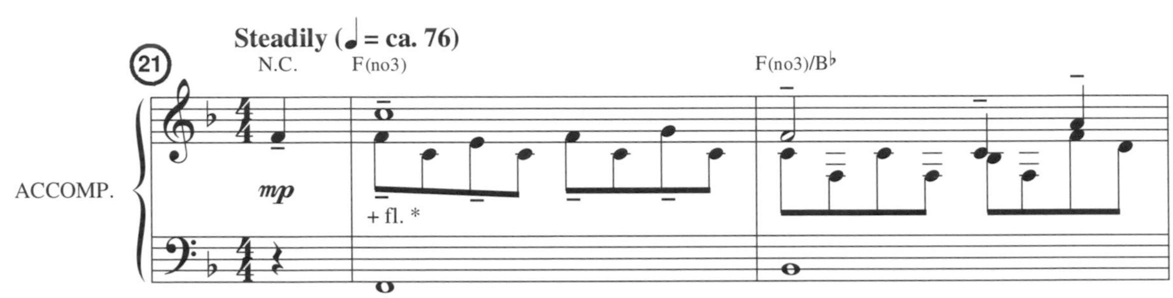

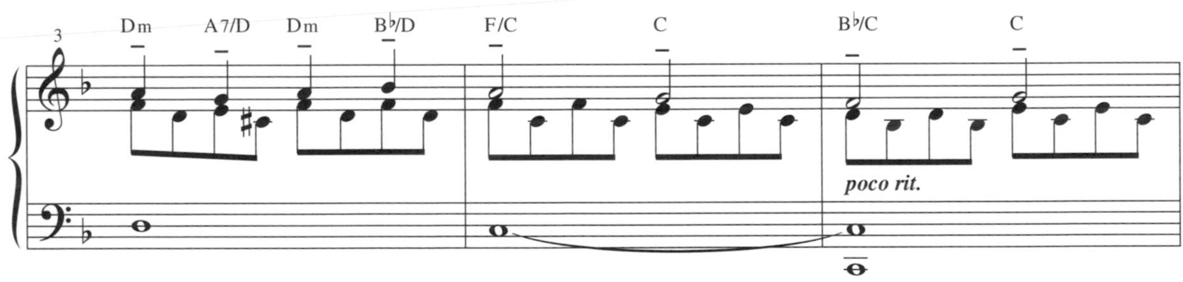

* Part for Flute (or other C-Instrument) is on pages 92-93.

8
o - pened my eyes, let me see. Beau - ty that made this
F C B♭2(no3) F C
11
heart a - dore You. Hope of a life spent with You.
Gm7 B♭ F C B♭(no3)
14
mf
15
Here I am to wor - ship. Here I am to bow down. Here I am to
N.C.
F Gm/F F F2 C/E Gm/E F/E C/E
- fl.

17
say that You're my God. You're al - to - geth - er love - ly, al - to - geth - er
F
B♭
F/B♭
C
F
Gm/F F
F2
+ fl.
20
wor - thy, al - to - geth - er won - der - ful to me.
22
C/E
Gm/E F/E
C/E
F
B♭(no3)
23
24
mf unis.
King of all days, oh, so high - ly ex - alt - ed,
F
Csus
Fsus/G
B♭(no3)
- fl.

26
mf
Hum - bly You came to
glo - rious in heav - en a - bove.
Hum - bly You came to the
F
C(no3)
B♭2(no3)
+ fl.
29
earth. All for love's sake be - came
earth You cre - at - ed. All for love's sake be-came poor.
Gm7
B♭
C/B♭
B♭Maj7
32
33
poor. Here I am to wor - ship. Here I am to bow down. Here I am to
B♭2
N.C.
Gm/F
F2
C/E
Gm/E F/E
- fl.

* Tune: ADESTE FILELES, John Francis Wade, 1711-1786
Words: Latin hymn, ascribed to John Francis Wade, 1711-1786

44
come, all ye faith - ful, joy - ful and tri -
F C F C/E F B♭/D
+ fl.
47
um - phant. O come ye, O come ye to
F/C C Gm7(♭5)/C♯ Dm C/E G C Dm C/E F
50
52
f
Beth - le - hem. Come and be -
C/G Dm/G C C/B♭ F/A C7/G F
- fl.
+ fl.

53
24
rit.
hold Him, born the King of an - gels.
C7/E F C/E A/C♯ Dm G/B C B♭/C C B♭/C C
- fl.
mf
+ fl.
rit. cresc.
57
58 Tempo I
f
Here I am to wor - ship. Here I am to bow down. Here I am to
C/D D Am/D G/D D G Am/G G G2 D/F♯ Am/D G/D D
60
say that You're my God. You're al - to - geth - er love - ly, al - to - geth - er
G G/B C Am/C G/C G/D D G Am/G G G2

63
wor - thy, al - to - geth - er won - der - ful to me.
D Am/D G/D D G G/B C
66
mf
67
Here I am to wor - ship. here I am to bow down. Here I am to
mf unis.
Come, all ye faith - ful,
C2 G D/F♯
mf - fl.
69
25
p unis.
say that You're my God. O
p
joy - ful and tri - um - phant.
G/B CMaj7 C6 C D/C C2(no3) N.C.
+ fl.
p - fl.

73
mp
mf
come, let us a - dore Him. O come, let us a - dore Him. O
G(no3)
G D/F♯ G D7/A G D/F♯ G
+ fl.
77
mp unis.
come, let us a - dore Him, Christ the
Am G D/F♯ C2/E D G/B C G/D D
- fl.
+ fl.
81
rit.
Lord.
N.C. G D7/G C/G C(no3)/D G
p

THE WATCHMAN:

Rejoice!
Jesus the Light of the World has come.
Behold, a brilliant star rises to light the way!
The night is ablaze with the glory of heaven.

Let the hungry come, for they will find the bread of life.

Let the thirsty come, for they will find streams of living water.

Let the weak come, for they will find the Mighty One of Israel.

Let the poor come, for they will find treasure more precious than gold.

Let the simple come, for they will find wisdom and knowledge.

Let the wise come, for they will find the heart of God.

Let all seekers come, for they will find rest from their wanderings.

Let all the people come and worship.

Come and find the One who is born King of kings and Lord of lords!

****

(optional alternative narration)

NARRATOR:
Jesus was born in the town of Bethlehem in Judea, during the time when Herod was king. Soon afterward, some men who studied the stars came from the East to Jerusalem and asked, "Where is the Baby born to be the king of the Jews? We saw His star when it came up in the east, and we have come to worship Him."

The star went ahead of them until it stopped over the place where the Child was. When they saw the Child with His mother Mary, they knelt down and worshiped Him. They brought out their gifts of gold, frankincense, and myrrh, and presented them to Him.
Matthew 2:1-2,10-11 (GNT)

ONE KING

Arranged by
MICHAEL BARRETT (BMI)
and DAVID ANGERMAN (ASCAP)

Words and music by
JEFF BORDERS, GAYLA BORDERS
and LOWELL ALEXANDER

* Part for Violin (or other C-Instrument) is on pages 90-91.

13
Sil - hou-ette of a car - a - van paint - ed a-gainst the sky;
Dm C Dm Am Dm C F
- vln.
+ vln.
17
27
end solo
wise men search - ing for the Ho - ly Child.
Gm Dsus Dm B♭ C Dm C
21
SOPRANO / ALTO
mp unis.
One king held the frank - in-cense. One king held the myrrh.
F C/E Dm Am
mp
- vln.
+ vln.
25
One king held the pur - est gold. One King held the hope of the
F C/E A B♭ C Am
- vln.

world.
TENOR / BASS
A
mf unis.
Dm C Dm C
+ vln.
star hangs o - ver Beth - le - hem. A jour - ney ends in the night.
Em D Em Bm Em D Em
Three kings trem - bling, be - hold the glor - ious sight.
Am Esus Em A#○ B
+ vln.
+ vln.

molto rit.
41
a tempo
unis.
Heav - en's trea - sure, Em - man - u - el,
unis.
Am/B Em/B B7
F♯m
E
F♯m
C♯m
a tempo
molto rit.
draw - ing men to bow down.
Ti - ny ba - by,
F♯m
E
F♯m
Bm
F♯sus
F♯m
49
born to wear a crown.
One king held the frank - in-cense.
D
E
F♯m
E
A
E/G♯
vln.

* Tune: GOD REST YE MERRY GENTLEMEN, Traditional English Melody
Words: Traditional English Carol

62
noth - ing you dis - may.
Re - mem - ber Christ our
D
C♯sus
C♯m
F♯m
+ vln.
65
Sav - ior was born on Christ - mas day
to
A/E
F♯m/E
D
C♯(no3)
C♯
68
30
save us all from Sa-tan's pow'r when we were gone a - stray.
Bm7
E7
A/C♯
C♯m
F♯m
D
C♯m7
Bm7
E
- vln.
+ vln.
mp

72
S.
mp unis.
A.
dim.
Oh, ti - ny Ba - by, born to wear a
N.C.
Bm7
F#4/2
F#m
D#○
dim.

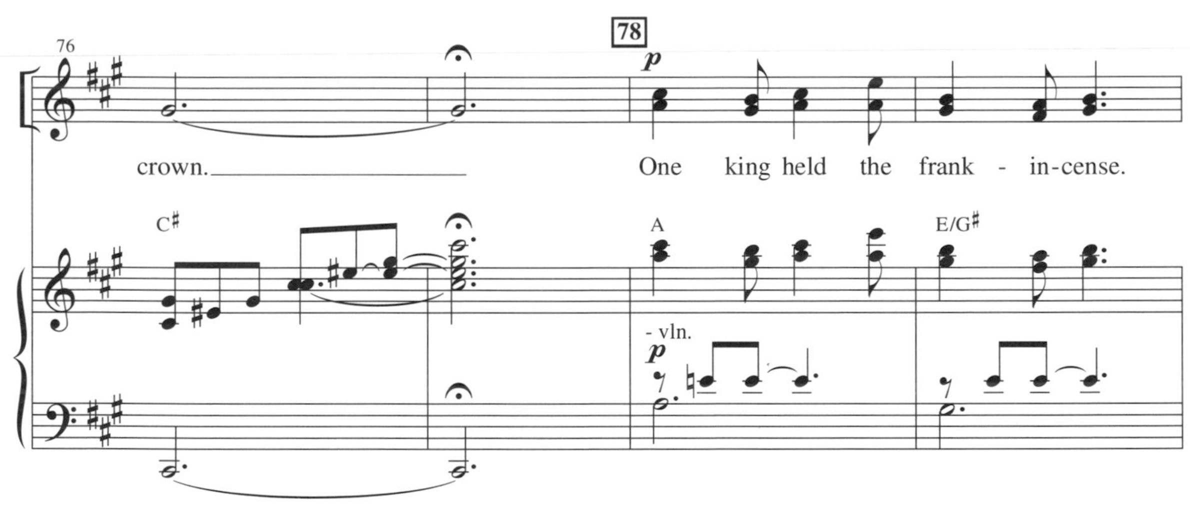
76
78
p
crown.
One king held the frank - in-cense.
C#
A
E/G#
- vln.
p

80
One king held the myrrh. One king held the pur - est gold.
F#m
C#m
A
E/G#
C#
+ vln.

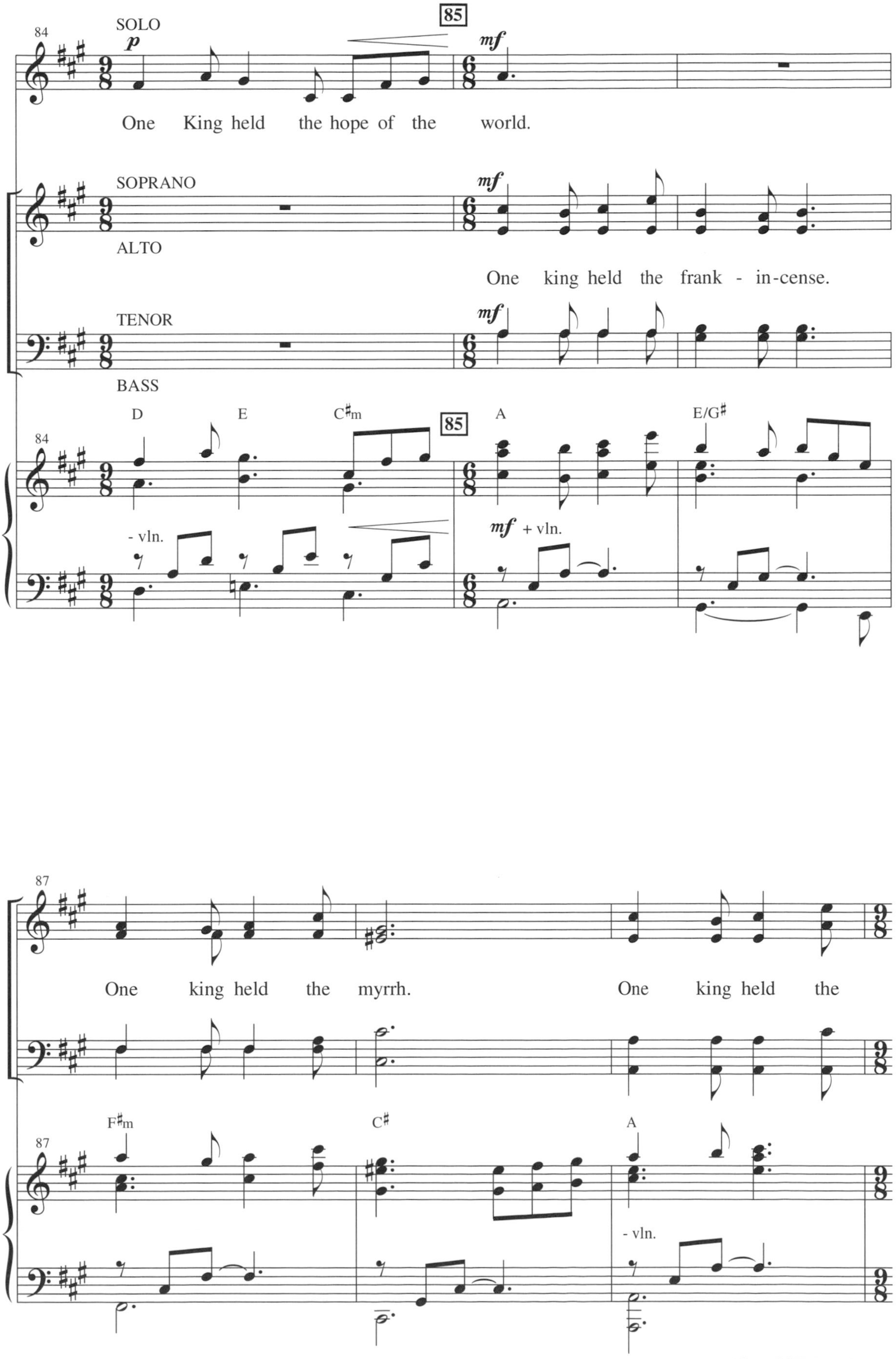

84 SOLO *p*
One King held the hope of the world.
85 *mf*

SOPRANO
ALTO
One king held the frank - in-cense.
TENOR
BASS

D E C♯m 85 A E/G♯
- vln. *mf* + vln.

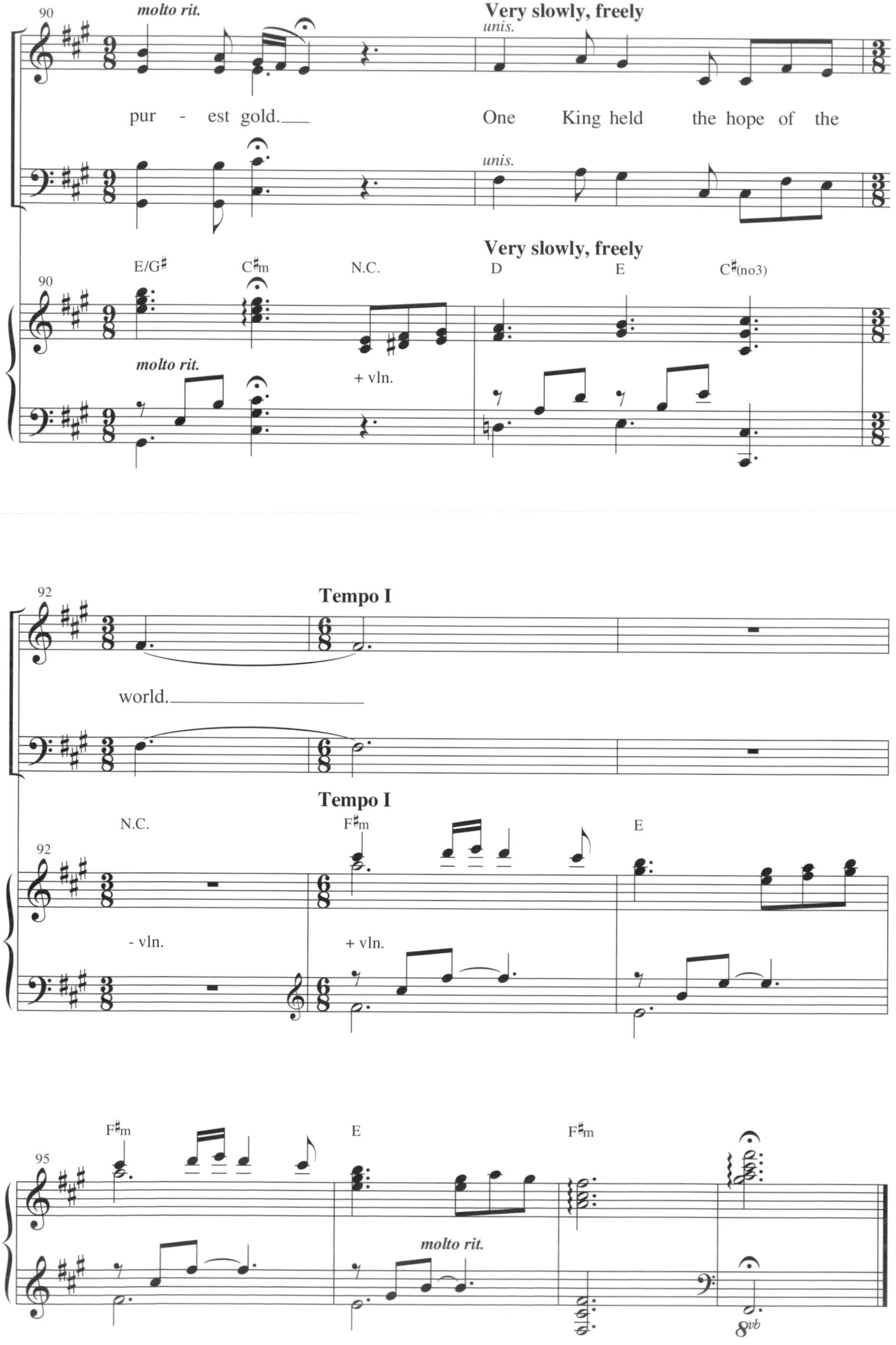

92
Tempo I
world.
Tempo I
N.C.
F♯m
E
92
- vln.
+ vln.

F♯m
E
F♯m
95
molto rit.
8vb

THE WATCHMAN:

Hear the word of the Lord…

I have set my watchmen upon thy walls, O Jerusalem,
which shall never hold their peace day nor night.

All you that make mention of the Lord, keep not silent.

Announce good tidings,
proclaim liberty,
and declare the dawn of salvation.

Christ is born!
Bethlehem's stable has become the palace of the King of kings!

Let the entire world rejoice
and make known the wonders of His Love!

****

(optional alternative narration)

NARRATOR:
In the beginning the Word already existed; the Word was with God, and the Word was God. From the very beginning the Word was with God. Through Him God made all things; not one thing in all creation was made without Him. The Word was the source of life, and this life brought light to people. The light shines in the darkness, and the darkness has never put it out.
John 1:1-5

LIGHT OF THE STABLE

Arranged by
DAVID ANGERMAN (ASCAP)

Words and music by
STEVE RHYMER
and ELIZABETH RHYMER

13
Hail, hail to the guid-ing light that brought us to-night to our
T. mf unis.
B.
B♭(no3) E♭ B♭ E♭ B♭
16
Sav - ior.
17
Hal - le!
Hal - le - lu - jah!
F B♭ E♭ B♭ F B♭
19
Hal - le!
Hal - le - lu - jah!
Hal - le!
Hal - le -
E♭ B♭ F B♭(no3) E♭ B♭ F

Ha - le - lu - jah!
- lu - jah!
Hal - le - lu - jah!
B♭
E♭
B♭
F
A♭
E♭
B♭
32
E♭/B♭
B♭
E♭/B♭
B♭
F
B♭

31
mp unis.
Come, now let it shine so bright to the know-ing Light of the
B♭
E♭
B♭
E♭
B♭
mp
34
sta - ble.
Kneel close to the Child so dear, Cast a -
mp unis.
F
B♭
E♭
B♭
37
side your fear and be thank - ful.
E♭
B♭
F
B♭

39
mf
Hail, hail to the new - born King! Let our
mf
39
E♭
A♭
E♭
mf
41
voic - es sing Him our prais - es! Hail, hail to the
41
A♭
E♭
A♭/E♭
E♭
B♭
E♭
44
guid - ing light that brought us to - night to our
44
A♭
E♭
A♭
E♭
A♭/E♭
E♭

46
47
Hal - le!
Sav - ior.
Hal - le - lu - jah!
Hal - le!
Hal - le - lu - jah!
46
B♭ E♭
47
A♭ E♭ B♭ E♭
49
Hal - le!
Hal - le!
Hal - le - lu - jah!
Hal - le-
Hal - le!
Hal - le!
Hal - le - lu - jah!
Hal - le-
49
A♭ E♭ B♭ E♭ A♭ E♭
52
Hal - le - lu - jah!
cresc.
- lu - jah!
Hal - le - lu - jah!
Hal - le - lu - jah!
cresc.
- lu - jah!
Hal - le - lu - jah!
52
B♭ E♭ A♭ E♭ B♭
cresc.

55
f
33
f
55
D♭
A♭
E♭
f
58
59
mf unis.
Hail, hail to the new-born King! Let our
mf unis.
58
59
F
B♭
F
mf
61
voic-es sing Him our prais - es! Hail, hail to the
61
B♭
F
C
F

64
guid - ing light that brought us to night to our
64
B♭
F
B♭
F
66
Hal - le!
67
Sav - ior.
Hal - le - lu - jah!
Hal - le!
Hal - le - lu - jah!
66
C
F
67
B♭
F
C
F
69
Hal - le!
Hal - le!
Hal - le - lu - jah!
Hal - le-
Hal - le!
Hal - le!
Hal - le - lu - jah!
Hal - le-
69
B♭
F
C
F
B♭
F

Hal - le - lu - jah!
cresc.
lu - jah!
Hal - le - lu - jah!
Hal - le - lu - jah!
cresc.
lu - jah!
Hal - le - lu - jah!
C
F
B♭
F
C
cresc.
f
f
E♭
B♭
F
f
Hal - le - lu - jah!
E♭
B♭

81
81
F
B♭
F
84
84
C
F
B♭
F
87
87
C
F

THE WATCHMAN:

I am the watchman.

From ancient times I have gazed into the night
seeking the assuring light of the morning.

I walked the ramparts of the city wall.
I shouted into the silence when danger threatened.

Now…all that has changed.

Jesus, the Light of the World was born.

Jesus, the Teacher lived.

Jesus, the Redeemer died.

Jesus, the Savior rose from the grave.

And Jesus, the King will come again.

I know that my Redeemer lives
and on the earth one day again will stand in all of His glory.

We will need no candle,
for Christ, Himself, will be our Light.

All is Well! All is Well!

****

(optional alternative narration)

NARRATOR:
So we are even more confident of the message proclaimed by the prophets. You will do well to pay attention to it, because it is like a lamp shining in a dark place until the Day dawns and the light of the morning star shines in your hearts.
2 Peter 1:19 (GNT)

ALL IS WELL

Arranged by
MICHAEL BARRETT (BMI)

Words and music by
MICHAEL W. SMITH
and WAYNE KIRKPATRICK

* Tune: THE FIRST NOEL, Traditional English Melody

13
re - joice,
An - gels and men re - joice, re - joice,
re - joice,
re - joice, re - joice,
Fm7 E♭/G Fm7 E♭/G D♭ B♭7sus B♭7
17
for to - night, dark - ness fell
E♭ E♭Maj7/G Cm C2 B♭6
21
in - to the dawn of love's light. Sing
mf
A♭ E♭/A♭ A♭ E♭/G A♭Maj7 E♭2/G

25
al - le, sing al - le - lu -
25
A♭Maj7
E♭2/G
G♭Maj7
D♭2/F
mf
29
35
ia!
29
A♭/B♭
B♭
A♭/B♭
B♭
A♭/B♭
B♭6
Fm/B♭
33
p
All is well. All is well.
p
p
33
E♭
A♭
A♭m
E♭
p

37
mp
on earth.
Let there be peace on earth, on earth.
mp
on earth.
on earth, on earth.
37
Fm7 E♭/G Fm7 E♭/G D♭ B♭sus7 B♭7
mp
41
Christ is come. Go and tell
41
E♭ E♭Maj7/G Cm C4/2 E♭Maj7/G E♭/G
45
mf
that He is in the man - ger. Sing
mf
45
A♭ E♭/A♭ A♭ E♭/G A♭Maj7 E♭2/G

49
unis.
al - le, sing al - le, al - le -
unis.
49
A♭Maj7
E♭2/G
G♭
D♭2/F
mf
53
36
allargando
lu - ia! Al - le - lu - ia!
53
B♭sus
B♭
A/B
B
A/B
allargando
57
Slower (♩ = ca. 84)
f
All is well! All is well!
f
57
Slower (♩ = ca. 84)
E
G♯m
A
B7
E
f

61
Lift up your voice and sing No - el!
F♯m7 E/G♯ A E/G♯ E D Bsus B
65
Born is now Em - man - u - el.
E G♯m A B7 E2 E
69
Born is our Lord and Sav - ior. Sing
unis.
F♯m E/G♯ C/G D

73
al - le - lu - ia! All is well! All is
C Em C/G D E D
77
well! All is well!
rit.
E D E
rit.
80
ff
All is well!
D Bm7 E

O SAVIOR OF OUR FALLEN RACE

OBOE
(or other C-Instrument)

Words and music by
KEITH *and* KRISTYN GETTY
Arranged by
DAVID ANGERMAN (ASCAP)

29
3
29-31
mf
36
39
f
2
40-41
f
43
46
mf
dim. poco a poco
51
52
mp
55
57
58
rit.
p
62
a tempo
dim. poco a poco al fine
66
pp

ONE KING

VIOLIN
(or other C-Instrument)

Words and music by
JEFF BORDERS, GAYLA BORDERS
and LOWELL ALEXANDER
Arranged by
MICHAEL BARRETT (BMI)
and DAVID ANGERMAN (ASCAP)

49
2
50-51
mf
55
f
60
2
61-62
f
66
68
3
68-70
mp
73
p
78
3
78-80
p
85
mf
89
molto rit.
Very slowly, freely
mp
93
Tempo I
mp
96
molto rit.
p

HERE I AM TO WORSHIP

(*with* "O Come, All Ye Faithful")

FLUTE
(or other C-Instrument)

Words and music by
TIM HUGHES
Incorporating
"O Come, All Ye Faithful"
Arranged by
DAVID ANGERMAN (ASCAP)

41
Faster, with a beat (♩ = ca. 98)
rit.
2
42-43
mf
mf
f
52
rit.
mf
f
Tempo I
58
67
3
67-69
mf
73
mp
p
mp
2
77-78
mp
rit.
p

PROMISES OF ISAIAH

FLUTES 1 & 2
(or other C-Instruments)

Music by
MICHAEL BARRETT (BMI)
and DAVID ANGERMAN (ASCAP)

3
35-37
mf
40
42
a la Baroque
mp
44
mp
48
mp
52
55
59
62
mf
65
67
f

70
70-71
75
(♮) (Fl. I only)
78
81
84
88
92
95
98
99-100
rit.
103